OTHER BOOKS BY JAMES CLAVELL:

WHIRLWIND

THRUMP-O-MOTO

THE CHILDREN'S STORY
...BUT NOT JUST FOR CHILDREN

NOBLE HOUSE

SHŌGUN

TAI-PAN

KING RAT

THE ART OF WAR

BY SUN TZU

Edited & with a Foreword by James Clavell

Delta

Published by
Dell Publishing
a division of
Bantam Doubleday Dell Publishing Group, Inc.
666 Fifth Avenue
New York, New York 10103

ISBN:0-385-29985-0

Reprinted by arrangement with Delacorte Press

Printed in the United States of America

September 1988

10 9 8 7 6 5 4

BG

CONTENTS

THE ART OF WAR

FOREWORD

Sun Tzu wrote this extraordinary book in China two and a half thousand years ago. It begins:

> The art of war is of vital importance to the state. It is a matter of life and death, a road either to safety or to ruin. Hence under no circumstances can it be neglected.

It ends:

> Hence it is only the enlightened ruler and the wise general who will use the highest intelligence of the army for purposes of spying, and thereby they achieve great results. Spies are a most important element in war, because upon them depends an army's ability to move.

I truly believe that if our military and political leaders in recent times had studied this work of genius, Vietnam could not have happened as it happened; we would not have lost the war in Korea (we lost because we did not achieve victory); the Bay of Pigs could not have occurred; the hostage fiasco in Iran would not have come to pass; the British Empire would not have been dismembered; and, in all probability, World Wars I and II would have been avoided—certainly they would not have been waged as they were waged, and the millions of youths obliterated unnecessarily and stupidly by monsters calling themselves generals would have lived out their lives.

Supreme excellence consists in breaking the enemy's resistance without fighting.

I find it astounding that Sun Tzu wrote so many truths twenty-five centuries ago that are still applicable today—especially in his chapter on the use of spies, which I find extraordinary. I think this little book shows clearly what is still being done wrong, and why our present opponents are so successful in some areas (Sun Tzu is obligatory reading in the Soviet political-military hierarchy and has been available in Russian for centuries; it is also, almost word for word, the source of all Mao Tse-tung's Little Red Book of strategic and tactical doctrine).

Even more importantly, I believe *The Art of War* shows quite clearly *how to take the initiative* and combat the enemy—any enemy.

Sun Tzu wrote: If you know the enemy and know yourself, you need not fear the result of a hundred battles.

Like Machiavelli's *The Prince* and Miyamoto Musashi's *The Book of Five Rings*, Sun Tzu's truths, contained herein, can equally show the

2

way to victory in all kinds of ordinary business conflicts, boardroom battles, and in the day to day fight for survival we all endure—even in the battle of the sexes! They are all forms of war, all fought under the same rules—*his rules*.

The first time I ever personally heard about Sun Tzu was at the races in Happy Valley in Hong Kong in 1977. A friend, P. G. Williams, a steward of the Jockey Club, asked me if I had ever read the book. I said no, and he told me that he would be happy to send me a copy the next day. When the book arrived, I left it unread. Then one day, weeks later, I picked it up. I was totally shocked that in all of my reading about Asia, about Japan and China particularly, I had not come across this book before. Since that time it has been a constant companion for me, so much so that during the course of the writing of *Noble House* many of the characters in it refer to Sun Tzu in all his glory. I think his work is fantastic. Hence this version of his book.

Unfortunately little is known of the man himself or of when he wrote the thirteen chapters. Some ascribe them to approximately 500 B.C. in the Kingdom of Wu, some to approximately 300 B.C.

About 100 B.C. one of his chroniclers, Su-ma Ch'ien, gives this biography:

> Sun Tzu, whose personal name was Wu, was a native of the Ch'i state. His *Art of War* brought him to the notice of Ho Lu, King of Wu. Ho Lu said to him, "I have carefully perused your thirteen chapters. May I submit your theory of managing soldiers to a slight test?"
>
> Sun Tzu replied, "You may."
>
> The king asked, "May the test be applied to women?"

The answer was again in the affirmative, so arrangements were made to bring 180 ladies out of the palace. Sun Tzu divided them into two companies and placed one of the king's favorite concubines at the head of each. He then made them all take spears in their hands and addressed them thus: "I presume you know the difference between front and back, right hand and left hand?"

The girls replied, "Yes."

Sun Tzu went on. "When I say 'eyes front,' you must look straight ahead. When I say 'left turn,' you must face toward your left hand. When I say 'right turn,' you must face toward your right hand. When I say 'about turn,' you must face right around toward the back."

Again the girls assented. The words of command having been thus explained, he set up the halberds and battle-axes in order to begin the drill. Then to the sound of drums he gave the order "right turn," but the girls only burst out laughing.

Sun Tzu said patiently, "If words of command are not clear and distinct, if orders are not thoroughly understood, then the general is to blame." He started drilling them again and this time gave the order "left turn," whereupon the girls once more burst into fits of laughter.

Then he said, "If words of command are not clear and distinct, if orders are not thoroughly understood, the general is to blame. But if his orders are *clear* and the soldiers nevertheless disobey, then it is the fault of their officers." So saying, he ordered the leaders of the two companies to be beheaded.

Now the King of Wu was watching from the top of a raised pavilion, and when he saw that his favorite concubines were about to be executed, he was greatly alarmed and hurriedly sent down the following message: "We are now quite satisfied as to our general's ability to handle troops. If we are bereft of these two concubines, our meat and drink will lose their savor. It is our wish that they shall not be beheaded."

Sun Tzu replied even more patiently: "Having once received His Majesty's commission to be general of his forces, there are certain commands of His Majesty which, acting in that capacity, I am unable to accept." Accordingly, and immediately, he had the two leaders beheaded and straightaway installed the pair next in order as leaders in their place. When this had been done the drum was sounded for the drill once more. The girls went through all the evolutions, turning to the right or to the left, marching ahead or wheeling about, kneeling or standing, with perfect accuracy and precision, not venturing to utter a sound.

Then Sun Tzu sent a messenger to the king saying: "Your soldiers, sire, are now properly drilled and disciplined and ready for Your Majesty's inspection. They can be put to any use that their sovereign may desire. Bid them go through fire and water and they will not now disobey."

But the king replied: "Let our general cease drilling and return to camp. As for us, we have no wish to come down and inspect the troops."

Thereupon Sun Tzu said calmly: "The king is only fond of words and cannot translate them into deeds."

After that the King of Wu saw that Sun Tzu was one who knew how to handle an army, and appointed him general. In the west Sun Tzu defeated the Ch'u state and forced his way into Ying, the capital; to the north he put fear into the states of Ch'i and Chin, and spread his fame abroad among the feudal princes. And Sun Tzu shared in the might of the kingdom.

So Sun Tzu became a general for the King of Wu. For almost two decades the armies of Wu were victorious over their hereditary enemies, the Kingdom of Yueh and Ch'u. Sometime within this period Sun Tzu died and his patron, the King of Wu, was killed in a battle. For a few years his descendants followed the precepts of Sun Tzu and continued to be victorious. And then they forgot.

In 473 B.C. the armies of Wu were defeated and the kingdom made extinct.

In 1782 *The Art of War* was first translated into French by a Jesuit, Father Amiot. There is a legend that this little book was Napoleon's key to success and his secret weapon. Certainly his battles depended upon mobility, and mobility is one of the things that Sun Tzu stresses. Certainly Napoleon used all of Sun Tzu to his own advantage to conquer most of Europe. It was only when he failed to follow Sun Tzu's rules that he was defeated.

The Art of War was not translated into English until 1905. The first English translation was by P. F. Calthrop. The second, the one that you will read here, is by Lionel Giles, originally published in Shanghai and London in 1910. I have taken a few liberties with this translation to make it a little more accessible—any translation from ancient Chinese to another language is to a certain extent a point of view—and have inserted some of Giles's notes, according to the Chinese method, immediately after the passages to which they refer.

I have also, for simplicity, deliberately eliminated all accents over Chinese names and places. It is, really, almost impossible to translate the Chinese sounds of a character into Roman lettering. Again, for simplicity, I've used the old-fashioned method of spelling. Let all scholars great and small please excuse me!

I sincerely hope you enjoy reading this book. Sun Tzu deserves to be read. I would like to make *The Art of War* obligatory study for all our serving officers and men, as well as for all politicians and all people in government and all high schools and universities in the free world. If I were a commander in chief or president or prime minister I would go further: I would have written into law that all officers, *particularly all generals*, take a yearly oral and written examination on these thirteen chapters, the passing mark being 95 percent—any general failing to achieve a pass to be automatically and summarily dismissed without appeal, and all other officers to have automatic demotion.

I believe, very much, that Sun Tzu's knowledge is vital to our survival. It can give us the protection we need to watch our children grow in peace and thrive.

Always remember, since ancient times, it has been known that . . . "the true object of war is *peace*."

JAMES CLAVELL

I

LAYING PLANS

Sun Tzu said:
The art of war is of vital importance to the state. It is a matter of life and death, a road either to safety or to ruin. Hence under no circumstances can it be neglected.

The art of war is governed by five constant factors, all of which need to be taken into account. They are: the Moral Law; Heaven; Earth; the Commander; Method and discipline.

The Moral Law causes the people to be in complete accord with their ruler, so that they will follow him regardless of their lives, undismayed by any danger.

Heaven signifies night and day, cold and heat, times and seasons.

Earth comprises distances, great and small; danger and security; open ground and narrow passes; the chances of life and death.

The Commander stands for the virtues of wisdom, sincerity, benevolence, courage, and strictness.

By *Method and discipline* are to be understood the marshaling of the army in its proper subdivisions, the gradations of rank among the officers, the maintenance of roads by which supplies may reach the army, and the control of military expenditure.

These five factors should be familiar to every general. He who knows them will be victorious; he who knows them not will fail.

Therefore, when seeking to determine your military conditions, make your decisions on the basis of a comparison in this wise:

Which of the two sovereigns is imbued with the Moral Law?

Which of the two generals has the most ability?

With whom lie the advantages derived from Heaven and Earth?

On which side is discipline most rigorously enforced?

> Tu Mu alludes to the remarkable story of Ts'ao Ts'ao (A.D. 155–220), who was such a strict disciplinarian that once, in accordance with his own severe regulations against injury to standing crops, he condemned himself to death for having allowed his horse to stray into a field of corn! However, in lieu of losing his head, he was persuaded to satisfy his sense of justice by cutting off his hair. "When you lay down a law, see that it is not disobeyed; if it is disobeyed, the offender must be put to death."

Which army is the stronger?

On which side are officers and men more highly trained?

In which army is there the most absolute certainty that merit will be properly rewarded and misdeeds summarily punished?

By means of these seven considerations I can forecast victory or defeat. The general who hearkens to my counsel and acts upon it will conquer—let such a one be retained in command! The general who hearkens not to my counsel nor acts upon it will suffer defeat—let such a one be dismissed! But remember: While heeding the profit of my counsel, avail yourself also of any helpful circumstances over and beyond the ordinary rules and modify your plans accordingly.

All warfare is based on deception. Hence, when able to attack, we must seem unable; when using our forces, we must seem inactive; when we are near, we must make the enemy believe we are far away; when far away, we must make him believe we are near. Hold out baits to entice the enemy. Feign disorder, and crush him. If he is secure at all points, be prepared for him. If he is in superior strength, evade him. If your opponent is of choleric temper, seek to irritate him. Pretend to be weak, that he may grow arrogant. If he is taking his ease, give him no rest. If his forces are united, separate them. Attack him where he is unprepared, appear where you are not expected.

The general who wins a battle makes many calculations in his temple before the battle is fought. The general who loses a battle makes but few calculations beforehand. Thus do many calculations lead to victory, and few calculations to defeat; how much more no calculation at all! It is by attention to this point that I can foresee who is likely to win or lose.

II

ON WAGING WAR

In the operations of war, where there are in the field a thousand swift chariots, ten thousand heavy chariots, and a hundred thousand mail-clad soldiers, with provisions enough to carry them a thousand *li*,* the expenditure at home and at the front, including entertainment of guests, small items such as glue and paint, and sums spent on chariots and armor, will reach the total of a thousand ounces of silver per day. Such is the cost of raising an army of a hundred thousand men.

When you engage in actual fighting, if victory is long in coming, the men's weapons will grow dull and their ardor will be dampened. If you lay siege to a town, you will exhaust your strength, and if the campaign is protracted, the resources of the state will not be equal to

---

* 2.78 modern *li* make a mile. The length may have varied slightly since Sun Tzu's time.

the strain. Never forget: When your weapons are dulled, your ardor dampened, your strength exhausted, and your treasure spent, other chieftains will spring up to take advantage of your extremity. Then no man, however wise, will be able to avert the consequences that must ensue.

Thus, though we have heard of stupid haste in war, cleverness has never been seen associated with long delays. In all history, there is no instance of a country having benefited from prolonged warfare. Only one who knows the disastrous effects of a long war can realize the supreme importance of rapidity in bringing it to a close. It is only one who is thoroughly acquainted with the evils of war who can thoroughly understand the profitable way of carrying it on.

The skillful general does not raise a second levy, neither are his supply wagons loaded more than twice. Once war is declared, he will not waste precious time in waiting for reinforcements, nor will he turn his army back for fresh supplies, but crosses the enemy's frontier without delay. The value of time—that is, being a little ahead of your opponent—has counted for more than either numerical superiority or the nicest calculations with regard to commissariat.

Bring war material with you from home, but forage on the enemy. Thus the army will have food enough for its needs. Poverty of the state exchequer causes an army to be maintained by contributions from a distance. Contributing to maintain an army at a distance causes the people to be impoverished.

On the other hand, the proximity of an army causes prices to go up; and high prices cause people's substance to be drained away. When their substance is drained away, they will be afflicted by heavy exactions. With this loss of substance and exhaustion of strength, the homes of the people will be stripped bare, and their incomes dissipated; at the same time government expenses for broken chariots, worn-out horses, breastplates and helmets, bows and arrows, spears and shields, protective mantlets, draught oxen and heavy wagons, will amount to almost half its total revenue.

A wise general makes a point of foraging on the enemy. One cartload of the enemy's provisions is equivalent to twenty of one's own, and likewise a single *picul* * of his provender is equivalent to twenty from one's own store.

Now, in order to kill the enemy, our men must be roused to anger. For them to perceive the advantage of defeating the enemy, they must also have their rewards. Thus, when you capture spoils from the enemy, they must be used as rewards, so that all your men may have a keen desire to fight, each on his own account.

Therefore in chariot fighting, when ten or more chariots have been taken, those should be rewarded who took the first. Our own flags should be substituted for those of the enemy, and the chariots mingled and used in conjunction with ours. The captured soldiers should be kindly treated and kept. This is called using the conquered foe to augment one's own strength.

In war, then, let your great object be victory, not lengthy campaigns. Thus it may be known that the leader of armies is the arbiter of the people's fate, the man on whom it depends whether the nation shall be in peace or in peril.

---

* A Chinese unit of weight equal to 133.33 pounds.

III

THE SHEATHED SWORD

To fight and conquer in all your battles is not supreme excellence; supreme excellence consists in breaking the enemy's resistance without fighting. In the practical art of war, the best thing of all is to take the enemy's country whole and intact; to shatter and destroy it is not so good. So, too, it is better to capture an army entire than to destroy it, to capture a regiment, a detachment, or a company entire than to destroy them.

Thus the highest form of generalship is to balk the enemy's plans; the next best is to prevent the junction of the enemy's forces; the next in order is to attack the enemy's army in the field; and the worst policy of all is to besiege walled cities, because the preparation of mantlets, movable shelters, and various implements of war will take up three whole months; and the piling up of mounds over against the walls will take three months more. The general, unable to control his irritation, will launch his men to the assault like swarming ants, with the result that one third of his men are slain, while the town still remains untaken. Such are the disastrous effects of a siege.

The skillful leader subdues the enemy's troops without any fighting; he captures their cities without laying siege to them; he overthrows their kingdom without lengthy operations in the field. With his forces intact he disputes the mastery of the empire, and thus, without losing a man, his triumph is complete.

This is the method of attacking by stratagem of using the sheathed sword.

It is the rule in war: If our forces are ten to the enemy's one, to surround him; if five to one, to attack him; if twice as numerous, to divide our army into two, one to meet the enemy in front, and one to fall upon his rear; if he replies to the frontal attack, he may be crushed from behind; if to the rearward attack, he may be crushed in front.

If equally matched, we can offer battle; if slightly inferior in numbers, we can avoid the enemy; if quite unequal in every way, we can flee from him. Though an obstinate fight may be made by a small force, in the end it must be captured by the larger force.

The general is the bulwark of the state: if the bulwark is strong at all points, the state will be strong; if the bulwark is defective, the state will be weak.

There are three ways in which a sovereign can bring misfortune upon his army:

By commanding the army to advance or to retreat, being ignorant of the fact that it cannot obey. This is called hobbling the army.

By attempting to govern an army in the same way as he administers a kingdom, being ignorant of the conditions that obtain in an army.

This causes restlessness in the soldiers' minds. Humanity and justice are the principles on which to govern a state, but not an army; opportunism and flexibility, on the other hand, are military rather than civic virtues.

By employing the officers of his army without discrimination, through ignorance of the military principle of adaptation to circumstances. This shakes the confidence of the soldiers.

> Su-ma Ch'ien about 100 B.C. added to this section: If a general is ignorant of the principle of adaptability, he must not be entrusted with a position of authority. The skillful employer of men will employ the wise man, the brave man, the covetous man, and the stupid man. For the wise man delights in establishing his merit, the brave man likes to show his courage in action, the covetous man is quick at seizing advantages, and the stupid man has no fear of death.

When the army is restless and distrustful, trouble is sure to come from the other feudal princes. This is simply bringing anarchy into the army, and flinging victory away. Thus we may know that there are five essentials for victory:

He will win who knows when to fight and when not to fight.

He will win who knows how to handle both superior and inferior forces.

He will win whose army is animated by the same spirit throughout all its ranks.

He will win who, prepared himself, waits to take the enemy unprepared.

He will win who has military capacity and is not interfered with by the sovereign.

If you know the enemy and know yourself, you need not fear the result of a hundred battles. If you know yourself but not the enemy, for every victory gained you will also suffer a defeat. If you know neither the enemy nor yourself, you will succumb in every battle.

IV

TACTICS

The good fighters of old first put themselves beyond the possibility of defeat, and then waited for an opportunity of defeating the enemy.

To secure ourselves against defeat lies in our own hands, but the opportunity of defeating the enemy is provided by the enemy himself. Hence the saying: One may *know* how to conquer without being able to *do* it.

Security against defeat implies defensive tactics; ability to defeat the enemy means taking the offensive. Standing on the defensive indicates insufficient strength; attacking, a superabundance of strength.

The general who is skilled in defense hides in the most secret recesses of the earth; he who is skilled in attack flashes forth from the topmost heights of heaven. Thus, on the one hand, we have ability to protect ourselves; on the other, to gain a victory that is complete.

To see victory only when it is within the ken of the common herd is not the acme of excellence. Nor is it the acme of excellence if you fight and conquer and the whole empire says, "Well done!" True excellence is to plan secretly, to move surreptitiously, to foil the enemy's intentions and balk his schemes, so that at last the day may be won without shedding a drop of blood. To lift an autumn hair is no sign of great strength; to see sun and moon is no sign of sharp sight; to hear the noise of thunder is no sign of a quick ear.

What the ancients called a clever fighter is one who not only wins, but excels in winning with ease. But his victories bring him neither reputation for wisdom nor credit for courage. For inasmuch as they are gained over circumstances that have not come to light, the world at large knows nothing of them, and he therefore wins no reputation for wisdom; and inasmuch as the hostile state submits before there has been any bloodshed, he receives no credit for courage.

He wins his battles by making no mistakes. Making no mistakes is what establishes the certainty of victory, for it means conquering an enemy that is already defeated.

Hence the skillful fighter puts himself into a position that makes defeat impossible and does not miss the moment for defeating the enemy. Thus it is that in war the victorious strategist only seeks battle after the victory has been won, whereas he who is destined to defeat first fights and afterward looks for victory. A victorious army opposed to a routed one is as a pound's weight placed in the scale against a single grain. The onrush of a conquering force is like the bursting of pent-up waters into a chasm a thousand fathoms deep.

The consummate leader cultivates the Moral Law and strictly adheres to method and discipline; thus it is in his power to control success.

So much for tactics.

V

ENERGY

The control of a large force is the same in principle as the control of a few men: it is merely a question of dividing up their numbers. Fighting with a large army under your command is nowise different from fighting with a small one: it is merely a question of instituting signs and signals.

To ensure that your whole host may withstand the brunt of the enemy's attack and remain unshaken, use maneuvers direct and indirect. In all fighting, the direct method may be used for joining battle, but indirect methods will be needed in order to secure victory.

Indirect tactics, efficiently applied, are as inexhaustible as Heaven and Earth, unending as the flow of rivers and streams; like the sun and moon, they end but to begin anew; like the four seasons, they pass away but to return once more.

There are not more than five musical notes, yet the combinations of these five give rise to more melodies than can ever be heard. There are not more than five primary colors, yet in combination they produce more hues than can ever be seen. There are not more than five cardinal tastes—sour, acrid, salt, sweet, bitter—yet combinations of them yield more flavors than can ever be tasted.

In battle, however, there are not more than two methods of attack—the direct and the indirect; yet these two in combination give rise to an endless series of maneuvers. The direct and the indirect lead on to each other in turn. It is like moving in a circle—you never come to an end. Who can exhaust the possibilities of their combination?

The onset of troops is like the rush of a torrent that will even roll stones along in its course. The quality of decision is like the well-timed swoop of a falcon that enables it to strike and destroy its victim. Therefore the good fighter will be terrible in his onset, and prompt in his decision.

Energy may be likened to the bending of a crossbow; decision, to the releasing of the trigger.

Amid the turmoil and tumult of battle, there may be seeming disorder and yet no real disorder at all; amid confusion and chaos, your array may be without head or tail, yet it will be proof against defeat. Simulated disorder postulates perfect discipline; simulated fear postulates courage; simulated weakness postulates strength. Hiding order beneath the cloak of disorder is simply a question of subdivision; concealing courage under a show of timidity presupposes a fund of latent energy; masking strength with weakness is to be effected by tactical dispositions.

Chang Yu relates the following anecdote of Liu Pang, the first Han emperor (256–195 B.C.): Wishing to crush the Hsiung-nu, he sent out spies to report on their condition. But the Hsiung-nu, forewarned, carefully concealed all their ablebodied men and well-fed horses, and only allowed infirm soldiers and emaciated cattle to be seen. The result was that the spies one and all recommended the emperor to deliver his attack. Lou Ching alone opposed them, saying: "When two countries go to war, they are naturally inclined to make an ostentatious display of their strength. Yet our spies have seen nothing but old age and infirmity. This is surely some *ruse* on the part of the enemy, and it would be unwise for us to attack." The emperor, however, disregarding this advice, fell into the trap and found himself surrounded at Po-teng.

Thus one who is skillful at keeping the enemy on the move maintains deceitful appearances, according to which the enemy will act. He sacrifices something that the enemy may snatch at it. By holding out baits, he keeps him on the march; then with a body of picked men he lies in wait for him.

In 341 B.C. the Ch'i state, being at war with Wei, sent T'ien Ch'i and Sun Pin against the general P'ang Chuan, who happened to be a deadly personal enemy of the latter. Sun Pin said: "The Ch'i state has a reputation for cowardice, and therefore our adversary despises us. Let us turn this circumstance to account." Accordingly, when the army had crossed the border into Wei territory, he gave orders to show 100,000 fires on the first night, 50,000 on the next, and the night after only 20,000. P'ang Chuan pursued them hotly, saying to himself: "I knew these men of Ch'i were cowards; their numbers have already fallen away by more than half." In his retreat, Sun Pin came to a narrow defile, which he calculated that his pursuers would reach after dark. Here he had a tree stripped of its bark, and inscribed upon it the words: "Under this tree shall P'ang Chuan die." Then, as night began to fall, he placed a strong body of archers in ambush nearby, with orders to shoot directly if they saw a light. Later on, P'ang Chuan arrived at the spot, and noticing the tree, struck a light in order to read what was written on it. His body was immediately riddled by a volley of arrows, and his whole army thrown into confusion.

The clever combatant looks to the effect of combined energy, and does not require too much from individuals. He takes individual talent into account, and uses each man according to his capabilities. He does not demand perfection from the untalented.

When he utilizes combined energy, his fighting men become, as it were, like rolling logs or stones. For it is the nature of a log or stone to remain motionless on level ground, and to move when on a slope; if four-cornered, to come to a standstill, but if round-shaped, to go rolling down. Thus the energy developed by good fighting men is as the momentum of a round stone rolled down a mountain thousands of feet in height. So much on the subject of energy.

VI

WEAK POINTS & STRONG

That the impact of your army may be like a grindstone dashed against an egg, use the science of weak points and strong.

Whoever is first in the field and awaits the coming of the enemy will be fresh for the fight; whoever is second in the field and has to hasten to battle will arrive exhausted. Therefore the clever combatant imposes his will on the enemy, but does not allow the enemy's will to be imposed on him. By holding out advantages to him, he can cause the enemy to approach of his own accord; or, by inflicting damage, he can make it impossible for the enemy to draw near. In the first case, he will entice him with a bait; in the second, he will strike at some important point that the enemy will have to defend.

If the enemy is taking his ease, harass him; if quietly encamped, force him to move; if well supplied with food, starve him out. Appear at points that the enemy must hasten to defend; march swiftly to places where you are not expected.

An army may march great distances without distress if it marches through country where the enemy is not. You can be sure of succeeding in your attacks if you only attack places that are undefended. You can ensure the safety of your defense if you only hold positions that cannot be attacked. That general is skillful in attack whose opponent does not know what to defend; and he is skillful in defense whose opponent does not know what to attack.

He who is skilled in attack flashes forth from the topmost heights of heaven, making it impossible for the enemy to guard against him. This being so, the places that he shall attack are precisely those that the enemy cannot defend. . . . He who is skilled in defense hides in the most secret recesses of the earth, making it impossible for the enemy to estimate his whereabouts. This being so, the places that he shall hold are precisely those that the enemy cannot attack.

O divine art of subtlety and secrecy! Through you we learn to be invisible, through you inaudible, and hence we can hold the enemy's fate in our hands. You may advance and be absolutely irresistible if you make for the enemy's weak points; you may retire and be safe from pursuit if your movements are more rapid than those of the enemy. If we wish to fight, the enemy can be forced to an engagement even though he be sheltered behind a high rampart and a deep ditch. All we need do is to attack some other place that he will be obliged to relieve. If the enemy is the invading party, we can cut his line of communications and occupy the roads by which he will have to return; if we are the invaders, we may direct our attack against the sovereign himself.

If we do not wish to fight, we can prevent the enemy from engaging us even though the lines of our encampment be merely traced out on the ground. All we need do is to throw something odd and unaccountable in his way.

> Tu Mu relates a stratagem of Chu-ko Liang, who in 149 B.C., when occupying Yang-p'ing and about to be attacked by Ssu-ma I, suddenly struck his colors, stopped the beating of the drums, and flung open the city gates, showing only a few men engaged in sweeping and sprinkling the ground. This unexpected proceeding had the intended effect; for Ssu-ma I, suspecting an ambush, actually drew off his army and retreated.

By discovering the enemy's dispositions and remaining invisible ourselves, we can keep our forces concentrated, while the enemy's must be divided. If the enemy's dispositions are visible, we can make for him in one body; whereas, our own dispositions being kept secret, the enemy will be obliged to divide his forces in order to guard against attack from every quarter. We can form a single united body, while the enemy must split up into fractions. Hence there will be a whole pitted against separate parts of a whole, which means that we shall be many to the enemy's few. And if we are able thus to attack an inferior force with a superior one, our opponents will be in dire straits.

The spot where we intend to fight must not be made known, for then the enemy will have to prepare against a possible attack at several different points; and his forces being thus distributed in many directions, the numbers we shall have to face at any given point will be proportionately few.

For should the enemy strengthen his van, he will weaken his rear; should he strengthen his rear, he will weaken his van; should he strengthen his left, he will weaken his right; should he strengthen his right, he will weaken his left. If he sends reinforcements everywhere, he will everywhere be weak.

Numerical weakness comes from having to prepare against possible attacks; numerical strength from compelling our adversary to make these preparations against us. Knowing the place and the time of the coming battle, we may concentrate from the greatest distances in order to fight. But if neither time nor place be known, then the left wing will be impotent to succor the right, the right equally impotent to succor the left, the van unable to relieve the rear, or the rear to support the van. How much more so if the farthest portions of the army are almost a hundred *li* apart, and even the nearest are separated by several *li*!

Though the enemy be stronger in numbers, we may prevent him from fighting. Scheme so as to discover his plans and the likelihood of their success. Rouse him, and learn the principle of his activity or inactivity. Force him to reveal himself, so as to find out his vulnerable spots. Carefully compare the opposing army with your own, so that you may know where strength is superabundant and where it is deficient.

In making tactical dispositions, the highest pitch you can attain is to conceal them; conceal your dispositions, and you will be safe from the prying of the subtlest spies, from the machinations of the wisest brains.

What the multitude cannot comprehend is how victory may be produced for them out of the enemy's own tactics.

All men can see the individual tactics necessary to conquer, but almost no one can see the strategy out of which total victory is evolved.

Military tactics are like unto water; for water in its natural course runs away from high places and hastens downward. So in war, the way is to avoid what is strong and to strike at what is weak. Water shapes its course according to the nature of the ground over which it flows; the soldier works out his victory in relation to the foe whom he is facing.

Therefore, just as water retains no constant shape, so in warfare there are no constant conditions. The five elements—water, fire, wood, metal, earth—are not always equally predominant; the four seasons make way for each other in turn. There are short days and long; the moon has its periods of waning and waxing. He who can modify his tactics in relation to his opponent, and thereby succeed in winning, may be called a heaven-born captain.

VII

MANEUVERING

Without harmony in the state, no military expedition can be undertaken; without harmony in the army, no battle array can be formed.

In war, the general receives his commands from the sovereign. Having collected an army and concentrated his forces, he must blend and harmonize the different elements thereof before pitching his camp.

After that comes tactical maneuvering, and there is nothing more difficult. The difficulty consists in turning the devious into the direct, and misfortune into gain. Thus, to take a long and circuitous route after enticing the enemy out of the way, and though starting after him to contrive to reach the goal before him, shows knowledge of the artifice of *deviation*.

Tu Mu cites the famous march of Chao She in 270 B.C. to relieve the town of O-yu, which was closely invested by a Ch'in army. The King of Chao first consulted Pien P'o on the advisability of attempting a relief, but the latter thought the distance too great, and the intervening country too rugged and difficult. His Majesty then turned to Chao She, who fully admitted the hazardous nature of the march, but finally said: "We shall be like two rats fighting in a hole—and the pluckier one will win!" So he left the capital with his army, but had only gone a distance of thirty *li* when he stopped and began throwing up entrenchments. For twenty-eight days he continued strengthening his fortifications, and took care that spies should carry the intelligence to the enemy. The Ch'in general was overjoyed, and attributed his adversary's tardiness to the fact that the beleaguered city was in the Han state, and thus not actually part of Chao territory. But the spies had no sooner departed than Chao She began a forced march lasting for two days and one night, and arrived on the scene of action with such astonishing rapidity that he was able to occupy a commanding position on the "north hill" before the enemy had got wind of his movements. A crushing defeat followed for the Ch'in forces, who were obliged to raise the siege of O-yu in all haste and retreat across the border.

Maneuvering with an army is advantageous; with an undisciplined multitude, most dangerous. If you set a fully equipped army to march in order to snatch an advantage, the chances are that you will be too late. On the other hand, to detach a flying column for the purpose involves the sacrifice of its baggage and stores.

Thus, if you order your men to roll up their buffcoats and make forced marches without halting day or night, covering double the usual distance at a stretch, and doing a hundred *li* in order to wrest an advantage, the leaders of all your three divisions will fall into the hands of the enemy. The stronger men will be in front, the jaded ones will fall behind, and on this plan only one-tenth of your army will reach its destination. If you march fifty *li* in order to outmaneuver the enemy, you will lose the leader of your first division, and only half your force will reach the goal. If you march thirty *li* with the same object, two-thirds of your army will arrive. An army without its baggage train is lost; without provisions it is lost; without bases of supply it is lost.

We cannot enter into alliances until we are acquainted with the designs of our neighbors. We are not fit to lead an army on the march unless we are familiar with the face of the country—its mountains and forests, its pitfalls and precipices, its marshes and swamps. We shall be unable to turn natural advantages to account unless we make use of local guides.

In war, practice dissimulation and you will succeed. Move only if there is a real advantage to be gained. Whether to concentrate or to divide your troops must be decided by circumstances. Let your rapidity be that of the wind, your compactness that of the forest. In raiding and plundering be like fire, in immovability like a mountain.

Let your plans be dark and impenetrable as night, and when you move, fall like a thunderbolt. When you plunder a countryside, let the spoil be divided among your men; when you capture new territory, cut it up into allotments for the benefit of the soldiery.

Ponder and deliberate before you make a move. He will conquer who has learned the artifice of deviation. Such is the art of maneuvering.

For as the ancient *Book of Army Management* says: On the field of battle, the spoken word does not carry far enough; hence the institution of gongs and drums. Nor can ordinary objects be seen clearly enough; hence the institution of banners and flags. Gongs and drums, banners and flags, are means whereby the ears and eyes of the host may be focused on one particular point. The host thus forming a single united body, it is impossible either for the brave to advance alone, or for the cowardly to retreat alone.

Tu Mu tells a story in this connection of Wu Ch'i, when he was fighting against the Ch'in state, approximately 200 B.C. Before the battle had begun, one of his soldiers, a man of matchless daring, sallied forth by himself, captured two heads from the enemy, and returned to camp. Wu Ch'i had the man instantly executed, whereupon an officer ventured to remonstrate, saying: "This man was a good soldier, and ought not to have been beheaded." Wu Ch'i replied: "I fully believe he was a good soldier, but I had him beheaded because he acted without orders."

This is the art of handling large masses of men.

In night fighting, then, make much use of signal fires and drums, and in fighting by day, of flags and banners, as a means of influencing the ears and eyes of your army.

A whole army may be robbed of its spirit; a commander in chief may be robbed of his presence of mind.

Li Ch'uan tells an anecdote of Ts'ao Kuei, a protégé of Duke Chuang of Lu. The latter state was attacked by Ch'i, and the duke was about to join battle after the first roll of the enemy's drums, when Ts'ao said: "Not just yet." Only after their drums had beaten for the third time did he give the word for attack. Then they fought, and the men of Ch'i were utterly defeated. Questioned afterward by the duke as to the meaning of his delay, Ts'ao Kuei replied: "In battle, a courageous spirit is everything. Now the first roll of the drum tends to create this spirit, but with the second it is already on the wane, and after the third it is gone altogether. I attacked when their spirit was gone and ours was at its height. Hence our victory. The value of a whole army—a mighty host of a million men—is dependent on one man alone: such is the influence of spirit!"

Now a soldier's spirit is keenest in the morning; by noonday it has begun to flag; and in the evening, his mind is bent only on returning to camp. A clever general, therefore, avoids an army when its spirit is keen, but attacks it when it is sluggish and inclined to return. This is the art of studying moods. Disciplined and calm, he awaits the appearance of disorder and hubbub among the enemy. This is the art of retaining self-possession.

To be near the goal while the enemy is still far from it, to wait at ease while the enemy is toiling and struggling, to be well fed while the enemy is famished—this is the art of husbanding one's strength. To refrain from intercepting an enemy whose banners are in perfect order, to refrain from attacking an army drawn up in calm and confident array—this is the art of studying circumstances.

It is a military axiom not to advance uphill against the enemy, nor to oppose him when he comes downhill. Do not pursue an enemy who simulates flight; do not attack soldiers whose tempers are keen. Do not swallow a bait offered by the enemy.

Do not interfere with an army that is returning home because a man whose heart is set on returning home will fight to the death against any attempt to bar his way, and is therefore too dangerous an opponent to be tackled.

When you surround an army, leave an outlet free. This does not mean that the enemy is to be allowed to escape. The object is to make him believe that there is a road to safety, and thus prevent his fighting with the courage of despair.

For you should not press a desperate foe too hard.

Ho Shih illustrates with a story taken from the life of Fu Yen-ch'ing. That general was surrounded by a vastly superior army of Khitans in the year A.D. 945. The country was bare and desertlike, and the little Chinese force was soon in dire straits for want of water. The wells they bored ran dry, and the men were reduced to squeezing lumps of mud and sucking out the moisture. Their ranks thinned rapidly, until at last Fu Yen-ch'ing exclaimed: "We are desperate men. Far better to die for our country than to go with fettered hands into captivity!" A strong gale happened to be blowing from the northeast and darkened the air with dense clouds of sandy dust. Tu Chung-wei was for waiting until this had abated before deciding on a final attack; but luckily another officer, Li Shou-cheng by name, was quicker to see an opportunity, and said: "They are many and we are few, but in the midst of this sandstorm our numbers will not be discernible; victory will go to the strenuous fighter, and the wind will be our best ally." Accordingly, Fu Yen-ch'ing made a sudden and wholly unexpected onslaught with his cavalry, routed the barbarians, and succeeded in breaking through to safety.

Such is the art of warfare.

VIII

VARIATION OF TACTICS

When in difficult country, do not encamp. In country where high roads intersect, join hands with your allies. Do not linger in dangerously isolated positions. In hemmed-in situations, you must resort to stratagem. In a desperate position, you must fight.

There are roads that must not be followed, towns that must not be besieged.

Almost twenty-two centuries ago, when invading the territory of Hsu-chou, Ts'ao Kung ignored the city of Hua-pi, which lay directly in his path, and pressed on into the heart of the country. This excellent strategy was rewarded by the subsequent capture of no fewer than fourteen important district cities. "No town should be attacked which, if taken, cannot be held, or if left alone, will not cause any trouble." Hsun Ying, when urged to attack Pi-yang, replied: "The city is small and well fortified; even if I succeed in taking it, it will be no great feat of arms; whereas if I fail, I shall make myself a laughingstock. It is a great mistake to waste men in taking a town when the same expenditure of soldiers will gain a province."

There are armies that must not be attacked, positions that must not be contested, commands of the sovereign that must not be obeyed.

The general who thoroughly understands the advantages that accompany variation of tactics knows how to handle his troops. The general who does not understand these may be well acquainted with the configuration of the country, yet he will not be able to turn his knowledge to practical account.

In A.D. 404, Liu Yu pursued the rebel Huan Hsuan up the Yangtze and fought a naval battle with him at the island of Ch'eng-hung. The loyal troops numbered only a few thousand, while their opponents were in great force. But Huan Hsuan, fearing the fate that was in store for him should he be overcome, had a light boat made fast to the side of his war junk, so that he might escape, if necessary, at a moment's notice. The natural result was that the fighting spirit of his soldiers was utterly quenched, and when the loyalists made an attack from windward with fireships, all striving with the utmost ardor to be first in the fray, Huan Hsuan's forces were routed, had to burn all their baggage, and fled for two days and nights without stopping.

In the wise leader's plans, considerations of advantage and of disadvantage will be blended together. If our expectation of advantage be tempered in this way, we may succeed in accomplishing the essential part of our schemes. If, on the other hand, in the midst of difficulties we are always ready to seize an advantage, we may extricate ourselves from misfortune.

Reduce the hostile chiefs by inflicting damage on them; make trouble for them, and keep them constantly engaged; hold out specious allurements, and make them rush to any given point.

> Chia Lin adds to this section several ways of inflicting this injury: "Entice away the enemy's best and wisest men, so that he may be left without counselors. Introduce traitors into his country, that the government policy may be rendered futile. Foment intrigue and deceit, and thus sow dissension between the ruler and his ministers. By means of every artful contrivance, cause deterioration among his men and waste of his treasure. Corrupt his morals by insidious gifts leading him into excess. Disturb and unsettle his mind by presenting him with lovely women."

The art of war teaches us to rely not on the likelihood of the enemy's not coming, but on our own readiness to receive him; not on the chance of his not attacking, but rather on the fact that we have made our position unassailable.

There are five dangerous faults that may affect a general, of which the first two are: recklessness, which leads to destruction; and cowardice, which leads to capture.

Next there is a delicacy of honor, which is sensitive to shame; and a hasty temper, which can be provoked by insults.

39

Yao Hsiang, when opposed in A.D. 357 by Huang Mei, Teng Ch'iang, and others, shut himself up behind his walls and refused to fight. Teng Ch'iang said: "Our adversary is of a choleric temper and easily provoked; let us make constant sallies and break down his walls, then he will grow angry and come out. Once we can bring his force to battle, it is doomed to be our prey." This plan was acted upon, Yao Hsiang came out to fight, was lured on as far as San-yuan by the enemy's pretended flight, and finally attacked and slain.

The last of such faults is oversolicitude for his men, which exposes him to worry and trouble, for in the long run the troops will suffer more from the defeat, or at best, the prolongation of the war, which will be the consequence.

These are the five besetting sins of a general, ruinous to the conduct of war. When an army is overthrown and its leader slain, the cause will surely be found among these five dangerous faults. Let them be a subject of meditation.

IX

THE ARMY ON THE MARCH

He who exercises no forethought but makes light of his opponents is sure to be captured by them. When encamping the army, pass quickly over mountains, and keep in the neighborhood of valleys.

Wu-tu Ch'iang was a robber captain in the time of the Later Han, approximately 50 A.D., and Ma Yuan was sent to exterminate his gang. Ch'iang having found a refuge in the hills, Ma Yuan made no attempt to force a battle, but seized all the favorable positions commanding supplies of water and forage. Ch'iang was soon in such a desperate plight for want of provisions that he was forced to make a total surrender. He did not know the advantage of keeping in the neighborhood of valleys.

Camp in high places facing the sun. Not on high hills, but on knolls or hillocks elevated about the surrounding country. Do not climb heights in order to fight.

After crossing a river, get far away from it. When an invading force crosses a river in its onward march, do not advance to meet it in midstream. It will be best to let half the army get across, and then deliver your attack.

> Li Ch'uan alludes to the great victory won by Han Hsin over Lung Chu at the Wei River in about 100 B.C.: "The two armies were drawn up on opposite sides of the river. In the night, Han Hsin ordered his men to take some ten thousand sacks filled with sand and construct a dam a little higher up. Then, leading half his army across, he attacked Lung Chu; but after a time, pretending to have failed in his attempt, he hastily withdrew to the other bank. Lung Chu was much elated by this unlooked-for success, and exclaiming, 'I felt sure that Han Hsin was really a coward!' he pursued him and began crossing the river in his turn. Han Hsin now sent a party to cut open the sandbags, thus releasing a great volume of water, which swept down and prevented the greater portion of Lung Chu's army from getting across. He then turned upon the force which had been cut off, and annihilated it, Lung Chu himself being among the slain. The rest of the army, on the farther bank, also scattered and fled in all directions."

If you are anxious to fight, do not go to meet the invader near a river he has to cross. Instead, moor your craft higher up than the enemy, and facing the sun. Do not move upstream to meet the enemy. Our fleet must not be anchored below that of the enemy, for then they would be able to take advantage of the current and make short work of you.

In crossing salt marshes, your sole concern should be to get over them quickly, without any delay, because of the lack of fresh water, the poor quality of the herbage, and last but not least, because they are low, flat, and exposed to attack. If forced to fight in a salt marsh, you should have water and grass near you, and get your back to a clump of trees.

In dry, level country, take up an easily accessible position with rising ground to your right and on your rear, so that the danger may be in front, and safety lie behind.

All armies prefer high ground to low, and sunny places to dark. Low ground is not only damp and unhealthy, but also disadvantageous for fighting. If you are careful of your men, and camp on hard ground, your army will be free from disease of every kind, and this will spell victory.

When you come to a hill or a bank, occupy the sunny side, with the slope on your right rear. It will be better for your soldiers and utilize the natural advantages of the ground.

When, in consequence of heavy rains up-country, a river which you wish to ford is swollen and flecked with foam, wait until it subsides. Country in which there are precipitous cliffs with torrents running between, deep natural hollows, confined places, tangled thickets, quagmires, and crevasses, should not be approached or else left with all possible speed. While we keep away from such places, we should get the enemy to approach them; while we face them, we should let the enemy have them on his rear.

If in the neighborhood of your camp there should be any hilly country, ponds surrounded by aquatic grass, hollow basins filled with reeds, or woods with thick undergrowth, they must be carefully routed out and searched; for these are places where men in ambush or insidious spies are likely to be lurking.

When the enemy is close at hand and remains quiet, he is relying on the natural strength of his position. When he keeps aloof and tries to provoke a battle, he is anxious for the other side to advance. If his place of encampment is easy of access, he is tendering a bait.

Movement among the trees of a forest shows that the enemy is advancing. If a scout sees that the trees of a forest are moving and shaking, he may know that they are being cut down to clear a passage for the enemy's march. The appearance of a number of screens in the midst of thick grass means that the enemy wants to make us suspicious.

The sudden rising of birds in their flight is the sign of an ambush at the spot below. Startled beasts indicate that a sudden attack is coming.

When there is dust rising in a high column, it is the sign of chariots advancing; when the dust is low, and spread over a wide area, it betokens the approach of infantry. When it branches out in different directions, it shows that parties have been sent to collect firewood. A few clouds of dust moving to and fro signify that the army is encamping.

Humble words and increased preparations are signs that the enemy is about to advance. Violent language and driving forward as if to the attack are signs that he will retreat. When the light chariots come out first and take up a position on the wings, it is a sign that the enemy is forming for battle. Peace proposals unaccompanied by a sworn covenant indicate a plot. When there is much running about and the soldiers fall into rank, it means that the critical moment has come. When some are seen advancing and some retreating, it is a lure.

In 279 B.C. T'ien Tan of the Ch'i state was hard pressed in his defense of Chi-mo against the Yen forces, led by Ch'i Chieh.

T'ien Tan openly said: "My only fear is that the Yen army may cut off the noses of their Ch'i prisoners and place them in the front rank to fight against us; that would be the undoing of our city."

The other side, being informed of this speech, at once acted on the suggestion; but those within the city were enraged at seeing their fellow countrymen thus mutilated, and fearing only lest they should fall into the enemy's hands, were nerved to defend themselves more obstinately than ever.

Once again T'ien Tan sent back converted spies who reported these words to the enemy: "What I dread most is that the men of Yen may dig up the ancestral tombs outside the town, and by inflicting this indignity on our forefathers cause us to become fainthearted."

Forthwith the besiegers dug up all the graves and burned the corpses lying in them. And the inhabitants of Chi-mo, witnessing the outrage from the city walls, wept passionately and were all impatient to go out and fight, their fury being increased tenfold.

T'ien Tan knew then that his soldiers were ready for any enterprise. But instead of a sword, he himself took a mattock in his hands, and ordered others to be distributed among his best warriors, while the ranks were filled up with their wives and concubines. He then served out all the remaining

rations and bade his men eat their fill. The regular soldiers
were told to keep out of sight, and the walls were manned
with the old and weaker men and with women. This done,
envoys were dispatched to the enemy's camp to arrange terms
of surrender, whereupon the Yen army began shouting for
joy. T'ien Tan also collected 20,000 ounces of silver from
the people, and got the wealthy citizens of Chi-mo to send
it to the Yen general with the prayer that, when the town
capitulated, he would not allow their homes to be plundered
or their women to be maltreated.

Ch'i Chieh, in high good humor, granted their prayer,
but his army now became increasingly slack and careless.
Meanwhile, T'ien Tan got together a thousand oxen, decked
them with pieces of red silk, painted their bodies, dragon-
like, with colored stripes, and fastened sharp blades on their
horns and well-greased rushes on their tails. When night
came on, he lighted the ends of the rushes and drove the
oxen through a number of holes that he had pierced in the
walls, backing them up with a force of 5,000 picked warriors. The animals, maddened with pain, dashed furiously
into the enemy's camp, where they caused the utmost confusion and dismay; for their tails acted as torches, showing
up the hideous pattern on their bodies, and the weapons on
their horns killed or wounded any with whom they came
into contact. In the meantime, the band of 5,000 had crept
up with gags in their mouths, and now threw themselves
on the enemy. At the same moment a frightful din arose
in the city itself, all those that remained behind making as
much noise as possible by banging drums and hammering
on bronze vessels, until heaven and earth were convulsed by
the uproar.

Terror-stricken, the Yen army fled in disorder, hotly

pursued by the men of Ch'i, who succeeded in slaying their general, Ch'i Chieh. The result of the battle was the ultimate recovery of some seventy cities that had belonged to the Ch'i state.

When the soldiers stand leaning on their spears, they are faint from want of food. If those who are sent to draw water begin by themselves drinking, the army is suffering from thirst. If the enemy sees an advantage to be gained and makes no effort to secure it, the soldiers are exhausted.

If birds gather on any spot, it is unoccupied: a useful way to tell that the enemy has secretly abandoned his camp.

Clamor by night betokens nervousness. Fear makes men restless, so they fall to shouting at night in order to keep up their courage. If there is disturbance in the camp, the general's authority is weak. If the banners and flags are shifted about, sedition is afoot. If the officers are angry, it means that the men are weary.

When an army feeds its horses with grain and kills its cattle for food, and when the men do not hang their cooking pots over the campfires, showing that they will not return to their tents, you may know that they are determined to fight to the death.

The rebel Wang Kuo of Liang was besieging the town of Ch'en-ts'ang, and Huang-fu Sung, who was in supreme command, and Tung Cho were sent out against him. Tung Cho pressed for hasty measures, but Sung turned a deaf ear to his counsel. At last the rebels were utterly worn out, and began to throw down their weapons of their own accord.

Sung was now for advancing to the attack, but Cho said:

"It is a principle of war not to pursue desperate men and not to press a retreating host."

Sung answered: "That does not apply here. What I am about to attack is a jaded army, not a retreating host; with disciplined troops I am falling on a disorganized multitude, not a band of desperate men." Thereupon he advanced to the attack, unsupported by his colleague, and routed the enemy, Wang Kuo being slain.

When envoys are sent with compliments in their mouths, it is a sign that the enemy wishes for a truce. If the enemy's troops march up angrily and remain facing ours for a long time without either joining battle or removing demands, the situation is one that requires great vigilance and circumspection.

To begin by bluster, but afterward to take fright at the enemy's numbers, shows a supreme lack of intelligence.

If our troops are no more in number than the enemy, that is amply sufficient; it only means that no direct attack can be made. What we can do is simply to concentrate all our available strength, keep a close watch on the enemy, and obtain reinforcements.

The sight of men whispering together in small knots or speaking in subdued tones points to disaffection among the rank and file. Too frequent rewards signify that the enemy is at the end of his resources, for when an army is hard pressed, there is always a fear of mutiny, and lavish rewards are given to keep the men in good temper. Too many punishments betray a condition of dire distress, because in such case discipline becomes relaxed, and unwonted severity is necessary to keep the men to their duty.

If soldiers are punished before they have grown attached to you, they will not prove submissive; and, unless submissive, they will be practically useless. If, when the soldiers have become attached to you, punishments are not enforced, they will still be useless. Therefore soldiers must be treated in the first instance with humanity, but kept under control by means of iron discipline. This is a certain road to victory.

> Yen Tzu (493 B.C.) said of Ssu-ma Jang-chu: "His civil virtues endeared him to the people; his martial prowess kept his enemies in awe. The ideal commander unites culture with a warlike temper; the profession of arms requires a combination of hardness and tenderness."

If, in training soldiers, commands are habitually enforced, the army will be well disciplined; if not, its discipline will be bad.

If a general shows confidence in his men but always insists on his orders being obeyed, the gain will be mutual. The art of giving orders is not to try to rectify the minor blunders and not to be swayed by petty doubts. Vacillation and fussiness are the surest means of sapping the confidence of an army.

X

TERRAIN

We may distinguish six kinds of terrain: accessible ground, entangling ground, temporizing ground, narrow passes, precipitous heights, positions at a great distance from the enemy.

Ground that can be freely traversed by both sides is called *accessible*. With ground of this nature, beat the enemy in occupying the raised and sunny spots, and carefully guard your line of supplies. Then you will be able to fight with advantage.

Ground that can be abandoned but is hard to reoccupy is called *entangling*. From a position of this sort, if the enemy is unprepared, you may sally forth and defeat him. But if the enemy is prepared for your coming, and you fail to defeat him, then, return being impossible, disaster will ensue.

When the position is such that neither side will gain by making the first move, it is called *temporizing* ground, and the situation remains at a deadlock. In a position of this sort, even though the enemy should offer an attractive bait, it will be advisable not to stir forth, but rather to retreat, thus enticing the enemy in his turn; then, when part of his army has come out, you may deliver your attack with advantage.

With regard to *narrow passes*, if you can occupy them first, let them be strongly garrisoned and await the advent of the enemy. Should the enemy forestall you in occupying a pass, do not go after him if the pass is fully garrisoned, but only if it is weakly garrisoned.

With regard to *precipitous heights*, if you precede your adversary, occupy the raised and sunny spots, and there wait for him to come up.

> Chang Yu tells the following anecdote of P'ei Hsing-chien (A.D. 619–682), who was sent on a punitive expedition against the Turkic tribes.
>
> At nightfall he pitched his camp as usual, and it had already been completely fortified by wall and ditch when suddenly he gave orders that the army should shift its quarters to a hill nearby. This was highly displeasing to his officers, who protested loudly against the extra fatigue that it would entail on the men. P'ei Hsing-chien, however, paid no heed to their remonstrances and had the camp moved as quickly as possible. The same night, a terrific storm came on, which flooded their former place of encampment to the depth of over twelve feet. The recalcitrant officers were amazed at the sight, and owned that they had been in the wrong.
>
> "How did you know what was going to happen?" they asked.
>
> P'ei Hsing-chien replied: "From this time forward be content to obey orders without asking unnecessary questions."

Remember, if the enemy has occupied precipitous heights before you, do not follow him, but retreat and try to entice him away.

With regard to *positions at a great distance from the enemy,* if the strength of the two armies is equal, it is not easy to provoke a battle, and fighting will be to your disadvantage.

Sometimes an army is exposed to calamities, not arising from natural causes, but from faults for which the general is responsible. These are: flight; insubordination; collapse; ruin; disorganization; rout.

Other conditions being equal, if one force is hurled against another ten times its size, the result will be the *flight* of the former.

When the common soldiers are too strong and their officers too weak, the result is *insubordination.*

> Tu Mu cites the unhappy case of T'ien Pu, who was sent to Wei in A.D. 821 with orders to lead an army against Wang T'ing-ts'ou. But the whole time he was in command, his soldiers treated him with the utmost contempt, and openly flouted his authority by riding about the camp on donkeys, several thousand at a time. T'ien Pu was powerless to put a stop to this conduct, and when, after some months had passed, he made an attempt to engage the enemy, his troops turned tail and dispersed in every direction. After that, the unfortunate man committed suicide by cutting his throat.

When the officers are too strong and the common soldiers too weak, the result is *collapse.*

When the higher officers are angry and insubordinate, and on meeting the enemy give battle on their own account from a feeling of resentment, before the commander in chief can tell whether or not he is in a position to fight, the result is *ruin*.

When the general is weak and without authority; when his orders are not clear and distinct; when there are no fixed duties assigned to officers and men, and the ranks are formed in a slovenly, haphazard manner, the result is utter *disorganization*.

When a general, unable to estimate the enemy's strength, allows an inferior force to engage a larger one, or hurls a weak detachment against a powerful one, and neglects to place picked soldiers in the front rank, the result must be a *rout*.

These are the six ways of courting defeat—neglect to estimate the enemy's strength; want of authority; defective training; unjustifiable anger; nonobservance of discipline; failure to use picked men—all of which must be carefully noted by the general who has attained a responsible post.

The natural formation of the country is the soldier's best ally; but a power of estimating the adversary, of controlling the forces of victory, and of shrewdly calculating difficulties, dangers, and distances, constitutes the test of a great general. He who knows these things, and in fighting puts his knowledge into practice, will win his battles. He who knows them not, nor practices them, will surely be defeated.

If fighting is sure to result in victory, then you must fight, even though the ruler forbid it; if fighting will not result in victory, then you must not fight, even at the ruler's bidding.

The general who advances without coveting fame and retreats without fearing disgrace, whose only thought is to protect his country and do good service for his sovereign, is the jewel of the kingdom.

Regard your soldiers as your children, and they will follow you into the deepest valleys; look on them as your own beloved sons, and they will stand by you even unto death.

Tu Mu tells of the famous general Wu Ch'i: He wore the same clothes and ate the same food as the meanest of his soldiers, refused to have either a horse to ride or a mat to sleep on, carried his own surplus rations wrapped in a parcel, and shared every hardship with his men. One of his soldiers was suffering from an abscess, and Wu Ch'i himself sucked out the virus. The soldier's mother, hearing this, began wailing and lamenting. Somebody asked her, "Why do you cry? Your son is only a common soldier, and yet the commander in chief himself has sucked the poison from his sore." The woman replied: "Many years ago, Lord Wu performed a similar service for my husband, who never left him afterward, and finally met his death at the hands of the enemy. And now that he has done the same for my son, he too will fall fighting I know not where."

If, however, you are indulgent, but unable to make your authority felt; kindhearted, but unable to enforce your commands; and incapable, moreover, of quelling disorder, then your soldiers must be likened to spoiled children; they are useless for any practical purpose.

Tu Mu writes: In A.D. 219, when Lu Meng was occupying the town of Chiang-ling, he had given stringent or-

54

ders to his army not to molest the inhabitants nor take anything from them by force. Nevertheless, a certain officer serving under his banner, who happened to be a fellow townsman, ventured to appropriate a bamboo hat belonging to one of the people, in order to wear it over his regulation helmet as a protection against the rain. Lu Meng considered that the fact of his being also a native of Ju-nan should not be allowed to palliate a clear breach of discipline, and accordingly he ordered his summary execution, the tears rolling down his face, however, as he did so. This act of severity filled the army with wholesome awe, and from that time forth even articles dropped in the highway were not picked up.

If we know that our own men are in a condition to attack, but are unaware that the enemy is not open to attack, we have gone only halfway toward victory. If we know that the enemy is open to attack, but are unaware that our own men are not in a condition to attack, we have gone only halfway toward victory. If we know that the enemy is open to attack, and also know that our men are in a condition to attack, but are unaware that the nature of the ground makes fighting impracticable, we have still gone only halfway toward victory.

The experienced soldier, once in motion, is never bewildered; once he has broken camp, he is never at a loss. Hence the saying: If you know the enemy and know yourself, your victory will not stand in doubt; if you know Heaven and know Earth, you may make your victory complete.

XI

THE NINE SITUATIONS

The art of war recognizes nine varieties of ground: dispersive ground; facile ground; contentious ground; open ground; ground of intersecting highways; serious ground; difficult ground; hemmed-in ground; desperate ground.

When a chieftain is fighting in his own territory, it is *dispersive ground,* so called because the soldiers, being near to their homes and anxious to see their wives and children, are likely to seize the opportunity afforded by a battle and scatter in every direction.

When he has penetrated into hostile territory, but to no great distance, it is *facile ground.*

Ground that is of great advantage to either side is *contentious ground.*

When Lu Kuang was returning from his triumphant expedition to Turkestan in A.D. 385, and had got as far as Iho, laden with spoils, Liang Hsi, administrator of Liang-chou, taking advantage of the death of Fu Chien, King of Ch'in, wanted to bar his way into the province.

Yang Han, governor of Kao-ch'ang, counseled Liang Hsi, saying: "Lu Kuang is fresh from his victories in the west, and his soldiers are vigorous and mettlesome. If we oppose him in the shifting sands of the desert, we shall be no match for him, and we must therefore try a different plan. Let us hasten to occupy the defile at the mouth of the Kao-wu pass, thus cutting him off from supplies of water, and when his troops are prostrated with thirst, we can dictate our own terms without moving. Or if you think that the pass I mention is too far off, we could make a stand against him at the I-wu pass, which is nearer. The cunning and resource of Tzu-fang himself would be expended in vain against the enormous strength of those two positions."

Liang Hsi, refusing to act on this advice, was overwhelmed and swept away by the invader.

Ground on which each side has liberty of movement is *open ground*.

Ground that forms the key to three contiguous states, so that he who occupies it first has most of the empire at his command, is *ground of intersecting highways*.

When an army has penetrated into the heart of a hostile country, leaving a number of fortified cities in its rear, it is *serious ground*.

Mountain forests, rugged steeps, marshes and fens—all country that is hard to traverse: this is *difficult ground*.

Ground that is reached through narrow gorges, and from which we can only retire by tortuous paths, so that a small number of the enemy would suffice to crush a large body of our men: this is *hemmed-in ground*.

Ground on which we can only be saved from destruction by fighting without delay: this is *desperate ground*.

On dispersive ground, therefore, fight not. On facile ground, halt not. On contentious ground, attack not.

On open ground, do not try to block the enemy's way. On ground of intersecting highways, join hands with your allies.

On serious ground, gather in plunder. In difficult ground, keep steadily on the march.

On hemmed-in ground, resort to stratagem.

On desperate ground, fight.

Those who were called skillful leaders of old knew how to drive a wedge between the enemy's front and rear; to prevent cooperation between his large and small divisions; to hinder the good troops from rescuing the bad, the officers from rallying their men. When the enemy's men were scattered, they prevented them from concentrating; even when their forces were united, they managed to keep them in disorder. When it was to their advantage, they made a forward move; when otherwise, they stopped still.

If asked how to cope with a great host of the enemy in orderly array and on the point of marching to the attack, say: "Begin by seizing something that your opponent holds dear; then he will be amenable to your will."

Rapidity is the essence of war. Take advantage of the enemy's unreadiness, make your way by unexpected routes, and attack unguarded spots.

In A.D. 227, Meng Ta, governor of Hsin-ch'eng under the Wei emperor, Wen Ti, was meditating defection to the

House of Shu, and had entered into correspondence with Chu-ko Liang, prime minister of that state. The Wei general Ssu-ma I was then military governor of Wan, and getting wind of Meng Ta's treachery, he at once set off with an army to anticipate his revolt, having previously cajoled him by a specious message of friendly import.

Ssu-ma's officers came to him and said: "If Meng Ta has leagued himself with Wu and Shu, the matter should be thoroughly investigated before we make a move."

Ssu-ma I replied: "Meng Ta is an unprincipled man, and we ought to go and punish him at once, while he is still wavering and before he has thrown off the mask."

Then, by a series of forced marches, he brought his army under the walls of Hsin-ch'eng within the space of eight days. Now Meng Ta had previously said in a letter to Chu-ko Liang: "Wan is 1,200 *li* from here. When the news of my revolt reaches Ssu-ma I, he will at once inform his Imperial Master, but it will be a whole month before any steps can be taken, and by that time my city will be well fortified. Besides, Ssu-ma I is sure not to come himself, and the generals that will be sent against us are not worth troubling about."

The next letter, however, was filled with consternation: "Though only eight days have passed since I threw off my allegiance, an army is already at the city gates. What miraculous rapidity is this!" A fortnight later, Hsin-ch'eng had fallen and Meng Ta had lost his head.

In A.D. 621, Li Ching was sent from K'uei-chou in Ssu-ch'uan to reduce the successful rebel Hsiao Hsien, who had set up as emperor at Ching-chou Fu in Hupeh. It was autumn, and the Yangtze being then in flood, Hsiao Hsien never dreamt that his adversary would venture to come down through the gorges, and consequently made no preparations. But Li Ching embarked his army without loss of time, and was just about to start when the other generals implored him to postpone his departure until the river was in a less dangerous state for navigation.

Li Ching replied: "To the soldier, overwhelming speed is of paramount importance, and he must never miss opportunities. Now is the time to strike, before Hsiao Hsien even knows that we have got an army together. If we seize the present moment when the river is in flood, we shall appear before his capital with startling suddenness, like the thunder that is heard before you have time to stop your ears against it. This is the great principle in war. Even if he gets to know of our approach, he will have to levy his soldiers in such a hurry that they will not be fit to oppose us. Thus the full fruits of victory will be ours."

All came about as he predicted, and Hsiao Hsien was obliged to surrender, nobly stipulating that his people should be spared and he alone suffer the penalty of death.

The following are the principles to be observed by an invading force. The farther you penetrate into a country, the greater will be the solidarity of your troops, and thus the defenders will not prevail against you. Make forays in fertile country in order to supply your army with food.

Carefully study the well-being of your men, and do not overtax them. Concentrate your energy and hoard your strength. Keep your army continually on the move, and devise unfathomable plans.

Ch'en recalls the line of action adopted in 224 B.C. by the famous general Wang Chien, whose military genius largely contributed to the success of the first Ch'en emperor. He had invaded the Ch'u state, where a universal levy was made to oppose him. But, being doubtful of the temper of his troops, he declined all invitations to fight and remained strictly on the defensive. In vain did the Ch'u general try to force a battle; day after day Wang Chien kept inside his walls and would not come out, but devoted his whole time and energy to winning the affection and confidence of his men. He took care that they should be well fed, sharing his own meals with them, provided facilities for bathing, and employed every method of judicious indulgence to weld them into a loyal and homogeneous body.

After some time had elapsed, he told certain persons to find out how the men were amusing themselves. The answer was that they were contending with one another in shot putting and long jumping. When Wang Chien heard that they were engaged in these athletic pursuits, he knew that their spirits had been strung up to the required pitch and that they were now ready for fighting. By this time the Ch'u army, after repeating their challenge again and again, had marched away eastward in disgust. Wang Chien immediately broke up his camp and followed them, and in the battle that ensued they were routed with great slaughter.

Shortly afterward, the whole of Ch'u was conquered by Wang Chien.

Throw your soldiers into positions whence there is no escape, and they will prefer death to flight. If they will face death, there is nothing they may not achieve. Officers and men alike will put forth their uttermost strength. Soldiers in desperate straits lose the sense of fear. If there is no place of refuge, they will stand firm. If they are in the heart of a hostile country, they will show a stubborn front. If there is no help for it, they will fight hard. Thus, without waiting to be marshaled, the soldiers will be constantly on the alert, and without waiting to be asked, they will do your will; without restrictions, they will be faithful; without giving orders, they can be trusted.

Prohibit the taking of omens, and do away with superstitious doubts. Then, until death itself comes, no calamity need be feared.

If soldiers are not overburdened with money, it is not because they have a distaste for riches; if their lives are not unduly long, it is not because they are disinclined to longevity.

On the day they are ordered out to battle, your soldiers may weep, some sitting up bedewing their garments, and some lying down letting the tears run down their cheeks, not because they are afraid, but because all have embraced the firm resolution to do or die. But let them once be brought to bay, and they will display the courage of a Chuan Chu or a Ts'ao Kuei.

Chuan Chu, a native of the Wu state and contemporary with Sun Tzu himself, was employed by Kung-tzu Kuang, better known as Ho Lu Wang, to assassinate his sovereign Wang Liao with a dagger that he secreted in the belly of a fish served up at a banquet. He succeeded in his attempt, but was immediately hacked to pieces by the king's bodyguard. This was in 515 B.C.

The other hero referred to, Ts'ao Kuei, performed the exploit that had made his name famous 166 years earlier in 681 B.C. Lu had been thrice defeated by Ch'i, and was just about to conclude a treaty surrendering a large slice of territory, when Ts'ao Kuei suddenly seized Huan Kung, the Duke of Ch'i, as he stood on the altar steps and held a dagger against his chest. None of the duke's retainers dared to move a muscle, and Ts'ao Kuei proceeded to demand full restitution, declaring that Lu was being unjustly treated because she was a smaller and weaker state.

Huan Kung, in peril of his life, was obliged to consent, whereupon Ts'ao Kuei flung away his dagger and quietly resumed his place amid the terrified assemblage without having so much as changed color.

As was to be expected, the duke wanted afterward to repudiate the bargain, but his wise old counselor, Kuan Chung, pointed out to him the danger of breaking his word, and the upshot was that this bold stroke regained for Lu the whole of what she had lost in three pitched battles.

The skillful tactician may be likened to the *shuai-jan*. Now the *shuai-jan* is a snake that is found in the Ch'ang mountains. Strike at its head, and you will be attacked by its tail; strike at its tail, and you will be attacked by its head; strike at its middle, and you will be attacked by head and tail both.

Asked if an army can be made to imitate the *shuai-jan*, answer yes. For the men of Wu and the men of Yueh are enemies; yet if they are crossing a river in the same boat and are caught by a storm, they will come to each other's assistance just as the left hand helps the right.

It is not enough to put one's trust in the tethering of horses and the burying of chariot wheels in the ground. It is not enough to render flight impossible by such mechanical means. You will not succeed unless your men have tenacity and unity of purpose, and above all, a spirit of sympathetic cooperation. This is the lesson which can be learned from the *shuai-jan*.

The principle on which to manage an army is to set up one standard of courage that all must reach.

How to make the best of both strong and weak is a question involving the proper use of ground.

The skillful general conducts his army just as though he were leading a single man by the hand.

It is the business of a general to be quiet and thus ensure secrecy; upright and just, and thus maintain order. He must be able to mystify his officers and men by false reports and appearances, and thus keep them in total ignorance.

In the year A.D. 88 Pan Ch'ao took the field with 25,000 men from Khotan and other central Asian states with the object of crushing Yarkand. The King of Kutcha replied by dispatching his chief commander to succor the place with an army drawn from the kingdoms of Wen-su, Ku-mo, and Wei-t'ou, totaling 50,000 men.

Pan Ch'ao summoned his officers and also the King of Khotan to a council of war, and said: "Our forces are now outnumbered and unable to make headway against the enemy. The best plan, then, is for us to separate and disperse, each in a different direction. The King of Khotan will march away by the easterly route, and I will then return myself toward the west. Let us wait until the evening drum has sounded and then start.

Pan Ch'ao now secretly released the prisoners whom he had taken alive, and the King of Kutcha was thus informed of his plans. Much elated by the news, the latter set off at once at the head of 10,000 horsemen to bar Pan Ch'ao's retreat in the west, while the King of Wen-su rode eastward with 9,000 horses in order to intercept the King of Khotan.

As soon as Pan Ch'ao knew that the two chieftains had gone, he called his divisions together, got them well in hand, and at cockcrow hurled them against the army of Yarkand, as it lay encamped. The barbarians, panic-stricken, fled in confusion, and were closely pursued by Pan Ch'ao. Over 5,000 heads were brought back as trophies, besides immense spoils in the form of horses and cattle and valuables of every description. Yarkand then capitulating, Kutcha and the other kingdoms drew off their respective forces. From that time forward, Pan Ch'ao's prestige completely overawed the countries of the west.

By altering his arrangements and changing his plans, the skillful general keeps the enemy without definite knowledge. By shifting his camp and taking circuitous routes, he prevents the enemy from anticipating his purpose. At the critical moment, the leader of an army acts like one who has climbed up a height and then kicks away the ladder behind him. He carries his men deep into hostile territory before he shows his hand. He burns his boats and breaks his cooking pots; like a shepherd driving a flock of sheep, he drives his men this way and that, and none knows whither he is going.

To muster his host and bring it into danger—this may be termed the business of the general.

The different measures suited to the nine varieties of ground; the expediency of aggressive or defensive tactics; and the fundamental laws of human nature: these are things that must most certainly be studied.

When invading hostile territory, the general principle is that penetrating deeply brings cohesion; penetrating but a short way means dispersion.

When you leave your own country behind, and take your army across neighboring territory, you find yourself on *critical ground*. When there are means of communication on all four sides, the ground is one of *intersecting highways*. When you penetrate deeply into a country, it is *serious ground*. When you penetrate but a little way, it is *facile ground*. When you have the enemy's strongholds on your rear, and narrow passes in front, it is *hemmed-in ground*. When there is no place of refuge at all, it is *desperate ground*.

On dispersive ground, inspire your men with unity of purpose. On facile ground, see that there is close connection between all parts of the army. On contentious ground, hurry up your rear guard. On open ground, keep a vigilant eye on your defenses, fearing a surprise attack.

On ground of intersecting highways, consolidate your alliances.

On serious ground, ensure a continuous stream of supplies. On difficult ground, keep pushing on along the road.

On hemmed-in ground, block any way of retreat to make it seem that you mean to defend the position, whereas your real intention is to burst suddenly through the enemy's lines.

In A.D. 532, Kao Huan, afterward emperor and canonized as Shen-wu, was surrounded by a great army under Ehr-chu Chao and others. His own force was comparatively small, consisting only of 2,000 horse and something under 30,000 foot. The lines of investment had not been drawn very closely together, gaps being left at certain points. But Kao Huan, instead of trying to escape, actually made a shift to block all the remaining outlets himself by driving into them a number of oxen and donkeys roped together. As soon as his officers and men saw that there was nothing for it but to conquer or die, their spirits rose to an extraordinary pitch of exaltation, and they charged with such desperate ferocity that the opposing ranks broke and crumbled under their onslaught.

On desperate ground, proclaim to your soldiers the hopelessness of saving their lives. The only chance of life lies in giving up all hope of it.

For it is the soldier's disposition to offer an obstinate resistance when surrounded, to fight hard when he cannot help himself, and to obey promptly when he has fallen into danger.

In A.D. 73, when Pan Ch'ao arrived at Shan-shan, Kuang, the king of the country, received him at first with great politeness and respect; but shortly afterward his behavior underwent a sudden change, and he became remiss and negligent.

Pan Ch'ao spoke about this to the officers of his suite: "Have you not noticed," he said, "that Kuang's polite intentions are on the wane? This must signify that envoys have come from the northern barbarians, and that consequently he is in a state of indecision, not knowing with which side to throw in his lot. That surely is the reason. The truly wise man, we are told, can perceive things before they have come to pass; how much more, then, those that are already manifest!"

Thereupon he called one of the natives who had been assigned to his service and set a trap for him, saying: "Where are those envoys from the Hsiung-nu who arrived some days ago?"

The man was so taken aback that between surprise and fear he presently blurted out the whole truth. Pan Ch'ao, keeping his informant carefully under lock and key, then summoned a general gathering of his officers, thirty-six in all, and began drinking with them. When the wine had mounted into their heads a little, he tried to rouse their spirit still further by addressing them thus: "Gentlemen, here we are in the heart of an isolated region, anxious to achieve riches and honor by some great exploit. Now it happens that an ambassador from the Hsiung-nu arrived in this kingdom only a few days ago, and the result is that the respectful courtesy extended toward us by our royal host has disappeared. Should this envoy prevail upon him to seize our party and hand us over to the Hsiung-nu, our bones will become food for the wolves of the desert. What are we to do?"

With one accord, the officers replied: *"Standing as we do in peril of our lives, we will follow our commander through life and death."*

We cannot enter into alliance with neighboring princes until we are acquainted with their designs. We are not fit to lead an army on the march unless we are familiar with the face of the country—its mountains and forests, its pitfalls and precipices, its marshes and swamps. We shall be unable to turn natural advantages to account unless we make use of local guides.

To be ignorant of any one of the following four or five principles does not befit a warlike prince.

When a warlike prince attacks a powerful state, his generalship shows itself in preventing the concentration of the enemy's forces. He overawes his opponents, and their allies are prevented from joining against him. In attacking a powerful state, if you can divide her forces, you will have a superiority in strength; if you have a superiority in strength, you will overawe the enemy; if you overawe the enemy, the neighboring states will be frightened; and if the neighboring states are frightened, the enemy's allies will be prevented from joining her.

Hence he does not strive to ally himself with all and sundry, nor does he foster the power of other states. He carries out his own secret designs, keeping his antagonists in awe. Thus he is able to capture their cities and overthrow their kingdoms.

Bestow rewards without regard to rule, issue orders without regard to previous arrangements, and you will be able to handle a whole army as though you had to do with but a single man. In order to prevent treachery, your arrangements should not be divulged beforehand. There should be no fixity in your rules and arrangements.

Confront your soldiers with the deed itself, never let them know your design. When the outlook is bright, bring it before their eyes, but tell them nothing when the situation is gloomy. Place your army in deadly peril, and it will survive; plunge it into desperate straits, and it will come through in safety.

In 204 B.C., Han Hsin was sent against the army of Chao, and halted ten miles from the mouth of the Chinghsing pass, where the enemy had mustered in full force. Here, at midnight, he detached a body of 2,000 light cavalry, every man of which was furnished with a red flag.

Their instructions were to make their way through narrow defiles and keep a secret watch on the enemy.

"When the men of Chao see me in full flight," Han Hsin said, "they will abandon their fortifications and give chase. This must be the sign for you to rush in, pluck down the Chao standards and set up the red banners of Han in their stead." Turning then to his other officers, he remarked: "Our adversary holds a strong position, and is not likely to come out and attack us until he sees the standard and drums of the commander in chief, for fear I should turn back and escape through the mountains."

So saying, he first of all sent out a division consisting of 10,000 men, and ordered them to form in line of battle with their backs to the River Ti.

Seeing this maneuver, the whole army of Chao broke into loud laughter. By this time it was broad daylight, and Han Hsin, displaying the generalissimo's flag, marched out of the pass with drums beating, and was immediately engaged by the enemy.

A great battle followed lasting for some time, until at length Han Hsin and his colleague Chang Ni, leaving drums and banners on the field, fled to the division on the river-bank, where another fierce battle was raging. The enemy rushed out to pursue them and to secure the trophies, thus denuding their ramparts of men, but the two generals succeeded in joining the other army, which was fighting with the utmost desperation.

The time had now come for the 2,000 horsemen to play their part. As soon as they saw the men of Chao following up their advantage, they galloped behind the deserted walls, tore up the enemy's flags, and replaced them with those of Han.

When the Chao army turned back from the pursuit, the sight of these red flags struck them with terror. Convinced that the Hans had got in and overpowered their king, they broke up in wild disorder, every effort of their leader to stay the panic being in vain.

Then the Han army fell on them from both sides and completed the rout, killing a great number and capturing the rest, among whom was King Ya himself.

After the battle, some of Han Hsin's officers came to him and said: "In *The Art of War* we are told to have a hill or tumulus on the right rear, and a river or marsh on the left front. You, on the contrary, ordered us to draw up our troops with the river at our back. Under these conditions, how did you manage to gain the victory?"

The general replied: "I fear you gentlemen have not studied *The Art of War* with sufficient care. Is it not written there: *'Place your army in deadly peril, and it will survive; plunge it into desperate straits and it will come through in safety'*? Had I taken the usual course, I should never have been able to bring my colleagues round. If I had not placed my troops in a position where they were obliged to fight for their lives, but had allowed each man to follow his own discretion, there would have been a general rout, and it would have been impossible to do anything with them."

The officers admitted the force of his argument, and said: "These are higher tactics than we should have been capable of."

For it is precisely when a force has fallen into harm's way that it is capable of striking a blow for victory.

Success in warfare is gained by carefully accommodating ourselves to the enemy's purpose. If the enemy shows an inclination to advance, lure him on to do so; if he is anxious to retreat, delay on purpose that he may carry out his intention.

By persistently hanging on the enemy's flank, we shall succeed in the long run in killing the commander in chief—a vital act in war.

On the day that you take up your command, block the frontier passes, destroy the official tallies, and stop the passage of all emissaries either to or from the enemy's country.

Be stern in the council chamber, so that you may control the situation.

If the enemy leaves a door open, you mush rush in.

Forestall your opponent by seizing what he holds dear, and subtly contrive to time his arrival on the ground.

Walk in the path defined by rule, and accommodate yourself to the enemy until you can fight a decisive battle.

At first, then, exhibit the coyness of a maiden, until the enemy gives you an opening; afterward emulate the rapidity of a running hare, and it will be too late for the enemy to oppose you.

XII

ATTACK BY FIRE

There are five ways of attacking with fire. The first is to burn soldiers in their camp; the second is to burn stores; the third is to burn baggage trains; the fourth is to burn arsenals and magazines; the fifth is to hurl dropping fire among the enemy.

While Pan Ch'ao was still in Shan-shan, determined to end the extreme peril caused by the arrival of the envoy from the northern barbarian, Hsiung-nu, he exclaimed to his officers: "Never venture, never win! Unless you enter the tiger's lair, you cannot get hold of the tiger's cubs. The only course open to us now is to make an assault by fire on the barbarians under cover of night, when they will not be able to discern our numbers. Profiting by their panic, we shall exterminate them completely; this will cool the king's courage and cover us with glory, besides ensuring the success of our mission."

The officers were eager to follow him but pointed out that it would be necessary to discuss the matter first with the chief minister.

Pan Ch'ao then fell into a passion: "It is today," he cried, "that our fortunes must be decided! The chief minister is only a humdrum civilian, who on hearing of our project will certainly be afraid, and everything will be brought to light. An inglorious death is no worthy fate for valiant warriors."

Accordingly, as soon as night came on, he and his little band quickly made their way to the barbarian camp. A strong gale was blowing at the time. Pan Ch'ao ordered ten of the party to take drums and hide behind the enemy's barracks, it being arranged that when they saw flames shoot up, they should begin drumming and yelling with all their might. The rest of his men, armed with bows and crossbows, he posted in ambuscade at the gate of the camp. He then set fire to the place from the windward side, whereupon a deafening noise of drums and shouting arose on the front and rear of the enemy, who rushed out pell-mell in frantic disorder. Pan Ch'ao slew three of them with his own hand, while his companions cut off the head of the envoy and thirty of his suite. The remainder, more than a hundred in all, perished in the flames.

On the following day, Pan Ch'ao went back and informed Kuo Hsun, the chief minister, of what he had done. The latter was greatly alarmed and turned pale. But Pan Ch'ao, divining his thoughts, said with uplifted hand: "Although you did not go with us last night, I should not think, sir, of taking sole credit for our exploit."

This satisfied Kuo Hsun, and Pan Ch'ao, having sent for Kuang, King of Shan-shan, showed him the head of the barbarian envoy. The whole kingdom was seized with fear and trembling, which Pan Ch'ao took steps to allay by issuing a public proclamation. Then, taking the king's son as hostage, he returned to make his report to his own king.

In order to carry out an attack with fire, we must have means available; the material for raising fire should always be kept in readiness.

There is a proper season for making attacks with fire, and special days for starting a conflagration. The proper season is when the weather is very dry; the special days are those when the moon is in the constellations of the Sieve, the Wall, the Wing, or the Crossbar, for these four are all days of rising wind.

In attacking with fire, one should be prepared to meet five possible developments. When fire breaks out inside the enemy's camp, respond at once with an attack from without. If there is an outbreak of fire, but the enemy's soldiers remain quiet, bide your time and do not attack. When the force of the flames has reached its height, follow it up with an attack, if that is practicable; if not, stay where you are. If it is possible to make an assault with fire from without, do not wait for it to break out within, but deliver your attack at a favorable moment.

When you start a fire, be to the windward of it. Do not attack from the leeward. If the wind is in the east, begin burning to the east of the enemy, and follow up the attack yourself from that side. If you start the fire on the east side, and then attack from the west, you will suffer in the same way as your enemy.

A wind that rises in the daytime lasts long, but a night breeze soon falls.

In every army, the five developments connected with fire must be known, the movements of the stars calculated, and a watch kept for the proper days.

Those who use fire as an aid to the attack show intelligence; those who use water as an aid to the attack gain an accession of strength. By means of water, an enemy may be intercepted, but not robbed of all his belongings.

Unhappy is the fate of one who tries to win his battles and succeed in his attacks without cultivating the spirit of enterprise, for the result is waste of time and general stagnation. The enlightened ruler lays his plans well ahead; the good general cultivates his resources. He controls his soldiers by his authority, knits them together by good faith, and by rewards makes them serviceable. If faith decays, there will be disruption; if rewards are deficient, commands will not be respected.

Move not unless you see an advantage; use not your troops unless there is something to be gained; fight not unless the position is critical. No ruler should put troops into the field merely to gratify his own spleen; no general should fight a battle simply out of pique. Anger may in time change to gladness; vexation may be succeeded by content. But a kingdom that has once been destroyed can never come again into being; nor can the dead ever be brought back to life.

Hence the enlightened ruler is heedful, and the good general full of caution. This is the way to keep a country at peace and an army intact.

XIII

THE USE OF SPIES

Raising a host of a hundred thousand men and marching them great distances entails heavy loss on the people and a drain on the resources of the state. The daily expenditure will amount to a thousand ounces of silver. There will be commotion at home and abroad, and men will drop down exhausted on the highways. As many as seven hundred thousand families will be impeded in their labor.

Hostile armies may face each other for years, striving for the victory that is decided in a single day. This being so, *to remain in ignorance of the enemy's condition, simply because one grudges the outlay of a hundred ounces of silver in honors and emoluments, is the height of inhumanity.*

One who acts thus is no leader of men, no present help to his sovereign, no master of victory. What enables the wise sovereign and the good general to strike and conquer, and achieve things beyond the reach of ordinary men, is *foreknowledge.* Now this foreknowledge cannot be elicited from spirits; it cannot be obtained inductively from experience, nor by any deductive calculation.

Knowledge of the enemy's dispositions can only be obtained from other men. Knowledge of the spirit world is to be obtained by divination; information in natural science may be sought by inductive reasoning; the laws of the universe can be verified by mathematical calculation; but the dispositions of the enemy are ascertainable through spies and spies alone.

Hence the use of spies, of whom there are five classes: local spies; internal spies; converted spies; doomed spies; surviving spies.

When these five kinds are all at work, none can discover the secret system. This is called "divine manipulation of the threads." It is the sovereign's most precious faculty.

Having *local spies* means employing the services of the inhabitants of a district. In the enemy's country, win people over by kind treatment, and use them as spies.

Having *inward spies* means making use of officials of the enemy. Worthy men who have been degraded from office, criminals who have undergone punishment; also, favorite concubines who are greedy for gold, men who are aggrieved at being in subordinate positions, or who have been passed over in the distribution of posts, others who are anxious that their side should be defeated in order that they may have a chance of displaying their ability and talents, fickle turncoats who always want to have a foot in each boat. Officials of these several kinds should be secretly approached and bound to one's interests by means of rich presents. In this way you will be able to find out the state of affairs in the enemy's country, ascertain the plans that are being formed against you and, moreover, disturb the harmony and create a breach between the sovereign and his ministers. But there is a necessity for extreme caution in dealing with inward spies.

Lo Shang, governor of I-chou, sent his general Wei Po to attack the rebel Li Hsiung of Shu in his stronghold at P'i. After each side had experienced a number of victories and defeats, the rebel leader Li Hsiung had recourse to the services of a certain Po-tai, a native of Su-tu. He began by having him whipped until the blood came, and then sent him off to his enemy Lo Shang, whom he was to delude by offering to cooperate with him from inside the city, and to give a fire signal at the right moment for making a general assault.

Lo Shang, believing the promises of this inward spy, marched out all his best troops, and placed General Wei and others at their head with orders to attack at Po-tai's bidding. Meanwhile, Li Hsiung had prepared an ambuscade, and Po-tai, having reared long scaling ladders against the city walls, now lighted the beacon fire. Not knowing they were betrayed, Wei's men raced up on seeing the signal and began climbing the ladders as fast as they could, while others were drawn up by ropes lowered from above. More than a hundred of the soldiers entered the city in this way, every one of whom was forthwith beheaded. The rebel leader Li Hsiung then charged with all his forces both inside and outside the city, and routed the enemy completely.

Having *converted spies* means getting hold of the enemy's spies and using them for our own purposes: by means of heavy bribes and liberal promises, detaching them from the enemy's service and inducing them to carry back false information as well as to spy in turn on their own countrymen.

Having *doomed spies* means doing certain things openly for purposes of deception, and allowing our own spies to know of them and, when betrayed, report them to the enemy. We do things calculated to deceive our own spies, who must be led to believe that they have been unwittingly disclosed. Then, when these spies are captured in the enemy's lines, they will make an entirely false report, and the enemy will take measures accordingly, only to find that we do something quite different. The spies will thereupon be put to death.

Surviving spies, finally, are those who bring back news from the enemy's camp. This is the ordinary class of spies, who should form a regular part of the army. *Your surviving spy must be a man of keen intellect, though in outward appearance a fool; of shabby exterior, but with a will of iron. He must be active, robust, endowed with physical strength and courage: thoroughly accustomed to all sorts of dirty work, able to endure hunger and cold, and to put up with shame and ignominy.*

Once the Emperor T'ai Tsu sent Ta-hsi Wu to spy upon his enemy, Shen-wu of Ch'i. Wu was accompanied by two other men. All three were on horseback and wore the enemy's uniform.

When it was dark, they dismounted a few hundred feet away from the enemy's camp and stealthily crept up to listen, until they succeeded in catching the passwords used by the army. Then they got on their horses again and boldly passed through the camp under the guise of night watchmen; and more than once, happening to come across a soldier who was committing some breach of discipline, they actually stopped to give the culprit a sound cudgeling!

Thus they managed to return with the fullest possible information about the enemy's dispositions, and received warm commendation from the emperor, who in consequence of their report was able to inflict a severe defeat on his adversary.

There must be no more intimate relations in the whole army than those maintained with spies. No other relation should be more liberally rewarded. In no other relation should greater secrecy be preserved.

Spies cannot be usefully employed without a certain intuitive sagacity. Before using spies we must assure ourselves as to their integrity of character and the extent of their experience and skill. A brazen face and a crafty disposition are more dangerous than mountains or rivers; it takes a man of genius to penetrate such.

They cannot be properly managed without benevolence and straightforwardness.

Without subtle ingenuity of mind, one cannot make certain of the truth of their reports.

Be subtle! be subtle! and use your spies for every kind of business.

If a secret piece of news is divulged by a spy before the time is ripe, he must be put to death together with the person to whom the secret was told.

Whether the object be to crush an army, to storm a city, or to assassinate an individual, it is always necessary to begin by finding out the names of the attendants, the aides-de-camp, the doorkeepers, and the sentries of the general in command. Our spies must be commissioned to ascertain these.

The enemy's spies who have come to spy on us must be sought

out, tempted with bribes, led away, and comfortably housed. Thus they will become converted spies and available for our service.

It is through the information brought by the converted spy that we are able to acquire and employ local and inward spies. We must tempt the converted spy into our service, because it is he who knows which of the local inhabitants are greedy of gain, and which of the officials are open to corruption.

It is owing to his information, again, that we can cause the doomed spy to carry false tidings to the enemy.

Lastly, it is by his information that the surviving spy can be used on appointed occasions.

The end and aim of spying in all its five varieties is knowledge of the enemy; and this knowledge can only be derived, in the first instance, from the converted spy. He not only brings information himself, but makes it possible to use the other kinds of spies to advantage. Hence it is essential that the converted spy be treated with the utmost liberality.

Of old, the rise of the Yin dynasty was due to I Chi, who had served under the Hsia. Likewise, the rise of the Chou dynasty was due to Lu Ya, who had served under the Yin.

Hence it is only the enlightened ruler and the wise general who will use the highest intelligence of the army for purposes of spying, and thereby they achieve great results.

Spies are a most important element in war, because upon them depends an army's ability to move.

In peace prepare for war, in war prepare for peace.
The art of war is of vital importance to the state.
It is a matter of life and death,
a road either to safety or to ruin.
Hence under no circumstances can it
be neglected. . . .